T0148519

Danger Zone

FALLING FROM WITHIN

Casey Johnson

WESTBOW
PRESS®
A DIVISION OF THOMAS NELSON
& ZONDERVAN

Scripture taken from the New King James Version. Copyright 1979, 1980,
1982 by Thomas Nelson, inc. Used by permission. All rights reserved.

Scripture taken from the Holman Christian Standard Bible ® Copyright ©
2003, 2002, 2000, 1999 by Holman Bible Publishers. All rights reserved.

WestBow Press books may be ordered through booksellers or by contacting:

WestBow Press
A Division of Thomas Nelson & Zondervan
1663 Liberty Drive
Bloomington, IN 47403
www.westbowpress.com
1 (866) 928-1240

Because of the dynamic nature of the Internet, any web addresses or
links contained in this book may have changed since publication and
may no longer be valid. The views expressed in this work are solely those
of the author and do not necessarily reflect the views of the publisher,
and the publisher hereby disclaims any responsibility for them.

Any people depicted in stock imagery provided by Thinkstock are models,
and such images are being used for illustrative purposes only.
Certain stock imagery © Thinkstock.

ISBN: 978-1-5127-0081-7 (sc)
ISBN: 978-1-5127-0083-1 (hc)
ISBN: 978-1-5127-0082-4 (e)

Print information available on the last page.

WestBow Press rev. date: 12/09/2015

I would like to dedicate this book to my late grandmother, Altha Wiggins. Little did I know that listening to her sing "Amazing Grace" on that old wood swing would have such an impact on my life. To God be the glory for her unshakable faith.

Table of Contents

Introduction

A friend recently had the opportunity to go on a once-in-a- lifetime hunt for an exotic animal. As I talked with him on the phone about the adventure, I could hear the excitement in his voice. I asked him several questions to better understand where he was going and what he was hunting. As he began to explain the terrain, I was caught by surprise at something he said. He would be hunting on a military base, and certain areas had to be avoided because of land mines.

I immediately imagined the worst possible scenario. What if someone traveled across the line into the danger zone? He assured me that these areas were marked off well enough that if visitors crossed the line it would be their own fault. Thankfully, he managed to return home from the journey without entering the danger zone.

As I think about my friend's hunting trip, I am reminded of the many churches that have crossed into the danger zone in the way they are representing Christ to this world. Many churches have begun to move away from the things of God to satisfy themselves. The Bible is clear that in the last days men will become lovers of themselves and fall away from the truth. We are seeing the effects of that in our churches today.

This process is generally hard to spot because it happens gradually over time. Therefore we need to watch for the warning signs and act before the land mines explode. Once they begin to explode, they could trigger a chain reaction of events that threaten to destroy the local church. Join me as we discover some of the danger zones that we must avoid at all cost to prevent the church's collapse from within.

Danger One

CHANGING THE CHARACTER OF GOD

It is no secret that we live in a complex culture. Political parties cannot seem to work together for the good of the people, and wars are being fought left and right. People struggle to make ends meet, and political correctness governs the political, personal, and cultural arenas.

We live in a world that forbids us to use the word *terrorist* to describe a man who shouts out his fidelity to a false god as he is shooting people. This makes the average human being's everyday struggles even more difficult. The saddest part is that this politically correct mentality has slowly crept into the body of Christ. The result is the effort to minimize the parts of God that we don't like and elevate the parts that we love.

The danger in doing this is that we will begin to teach people about a god who does not exist—a god who looks, thinks, and acts just like them. I call this practice changing the character of God. The question is, Has changing the character of God started changing the character of our churches?

I cannot definitively say that this mentality has affected every church, but it has affected many. Those churches are heading down a road that leads away from God, not toward Him. The attempt to change the character of God is dangerous and can destroy our churches.

> Has changing the character of God started changing the character of our churches?

How does it happen?

How does this dangerous mentality find its way into our churches? We can look at Scripture to see one of the telltale signs of the beginning of this process. Let's return to the beginning of time and the life of Adam and Eve. The Bible teaches us in Genesis 1–2 that God created man from the dust of the earth, breathed life into him, and walked daily in fellowship with him. At this point, man was in a pretty good place. He was in a garden of paradise with a perfect woman and fruit that tasted as good as a rib-eye steak, and he got to walk and talk with God every day. What more could a guy want?

Apparently, Adam wanted more, but what? Tucked away deep in the garden was a tree containing a fruit that would give him knowledge of all things good and evil. This tree and the desire for its fruit would be Adam's downfall. God told Adam and Eve not to eat this fruit. Satan would use it to deceive them. Genesis 3:1–7 says,

Now the serpent was more cunning than any beast of the field which the Lord God had made. And he said to the woman, "Has God indeed said, 'You shall not eat of every tree in the garden'?" And the woman said to the serpent, "We may eat of the fruit of the trees of the garden; but of the fruit of the tree in the midst of the garden, God has said, 'You shall not eat of it, nor shall you touch it, lest you die.'" Then the serpent said to the woman, "You will not surely die. For God knows that in the day you eat of it your eyes will be opened, and you will be like God, knowing good and evil." So when the woman saw that the tree was good for food, that it was pleasant to the eyes, and a tree desirable to make one wise, she took of its fruit and ate. She also gave to her husband with her, and he ate. Then the eyes of both of them were opened, and they knew they were naked.

This passage shows how people who have fellowship with God can be deceived into adopting a dangerous mind-set that will destroy them. The reason Adam and Eve fell is found in verse 5: "For God knows that in the day you eat of it your eyes will be opened, and you will be like God, knowing good and evil." Adam and Eve apparently wanted to be deities. This desire was rooted in their wish to please themselves. They had forsaken the wisdom of God to satisfy their own desire. They made earth and heaven about them instead of about God. Satan managed to convince Adam and Eve to forsake their Creator by getting them to focus on themselves.

That is what Satan does best. He convinces us to make this life about us instead of about God. Once you begin to make life about you, the God-given truths that once directed you will be compromised according to your desires.

> Satan managed to convince Adam and Eve to forsake their Creator by getting them to focus on themselves.

Just as it was in the garden of Eden, so it is in the body of Christ today. The danger of selfishness is lurking around every corner, at every business meeting, in every staff position, and in every encounter. How does a church begin to change the character of God and walk down the road of destruction? By eating the fruit of selfishness and making everything about its members.

Once a person begins to focus on himself, God goes and His truth along with Him. A person does not change the character of God on purpose, but selfishness is a prerequisite for doing this. Selfishness leads to creating a god that looks just like the person contriving the image.

A sovereign, powerful, just God becomes a tolerant God who bows to a person's every desire.

On one occasion, I was counseling a lady who said she felt that God wanted her to divorce her husband. When I told her that Scripture says God allows divorce only in adulterous situations (an exception that did not apply in this case), she began to completely change the character of God to make it seem that He thought like her. Suddenly, Scripture did not matter, and God didn't matter; only she mattered. Do you see how that works? It is dangerous.

Love or justice?

Now that we understand how this happens, let's take a look at how this mind-set is affecting the church. When you change the character of God, you are attacking His attributes. God's attributes are as significant as God Himself because they describe who He is. A basic principle taught in law school is that if you want to discredit a witness, you must attack his character. That is because his character speaks to what kind of person he is. What kind of person he is will determine what he is capable of doing. Therefore, if you want to make God capable of doing what you want Him to do, you must change His character by changing His attributes.

It is important to understand that all of God's attributes are equally important. Eliminate any one of them, and God ceases to be God. That is why it is important for the church to guard the character of God to its death. One attribute of God seems to be attacked more than any other. While many of you will probably point to the justice of God, the attribute attacked most is the love of God.

This may startle many of you. You may ask, how could the love of God be attacked by anyone? This is a reasonable question, since all people default to the love of God when they need something, a loved one dies, or they are at the ends of their ropes. In fact, the love of God is being attacked more than any His attributes because it is being exalted above all other attributes. To exalt the love of God in an unhealthy way is unbearable. Furthermore, it is damaging to the church.

Let's use a fictitious character named Ned to understand this truth. Ned is a nonbeliever who has been plagued with the sin of homosexuality for years. His attraction for the same sex has led him down an immoral road that is unhealthy for him and society. Visiting a local church one day, Ned is confronted with the truth of his sin. The pastor preaches a message from the Word of God on the sin of homosexuality, not screaming about how wrong it is but citing Scripture at length with a heart longing to see repentance.

Ned talks with the pastor and says he does not think that a loving God would punish him for expressing his feelings in the way he does. Ned says God just wants him to be happy. The pastor (politely) shares more Scripture with Ned about how God is a loving God, but He is also a just God and cannot let any of us get away with our sin. He then tells Ned how Jesus paid the price for his sin and wants him to turn from himself and follow Him. Ned is offended and leaves.

You may think I am about to declare that Ned is abusing God's love by exalting it over His justice. However, I am not. Ned is lost and won't understand the truth until his eyes are opened to his sin. Ned is not a danger to the church; he is not even a part of the church yet.

Let's continue the story. After Ned rushes out, his mother, a devout member of the church who was saved twenty-five years ago, approaches the pastor, furious about the meeting. She tells the pastor that he shouldn't have lectured Ned about the justice of God. She says he has scared Ned away and he will never come back. She says she does not think God will punish her son for being confused about his lifestyle choices. She says his homosexuality isn't the end of the world and he's a lot better than most people.

Ned's mom, the Christian, has just assaulted the love of God by exalting it over His justice. You can understand her concern for her son and his well-being. But she cannot change the character of God to dismiss sin. God is who He is, and there is no changing that. This may be a fictitious story, but pastors face similar situations every day. The truth is that when we exalt God's love over all His other attributes, we wage an all-out assault on the character of God. Exalting the love of God over other attributes is highly dangerous and will leave people in their sin.

The second-most attacked attribute of God is His justice. Justice means that God is right and acts according to truth without partiality. Most people do not like God's justice because of the word *hell*. No one wants to go to hell or have family or friends go there. People who desire to change the character of God constantly say, "A loving God would never send people to hell." This mentality leads people to exalt God's love and diminish His justice. Following this logic, no one is ever held accountable for anything.

If God doesn't judge people, then people are their own judges and can do whatever they desire. That sure plays into the hands of those who think life is all about them. When you diminish God's justice, you end up with a church where anything goes, because a loving, pushover god allows people to follow their convictions without consequences. This is exactly the kind of god they are looking for—one who looks just like them. This philosophy may jibe with the political correctness of the day, but it doesn't follow the Word of God.

One must understand that all of God's attributes are equal and give us a distinct picture of who He is. None of them can ever be compromised.

Early signs

We have seen the danger of changing the character of God. People change the character of God because they want to be God. This leads to a church that desires only to satisfy itself. There are several early warning signs of this problem.

The first sign is a diminishing stress on our dependence on God. Man will begin to put more emphasis on his accomplishments than on God's faithfulness. Man's resources become the focus in getting things done. You might ask how this is noticeable if God blesses man with resources to use for His glory. It's pretty simple. When the resources are not there, nothing is done. You may have heard it said that "we cannot do this, because we do not have the resources." A church has entered the early stage of selfishness when it begins to forget God is its resource.

Second, people will use the word *I* more often. This will happen from the pulpit to the congregation. When *I* is used frequently, then *I* starts to matter. This mentality runs contrary to Scripture. The Bible says in Luke 9:23, "If any man desires to come after me, he must deny himself and take up his cross daily and follow me." A person cannot deny himself and follow

> A church has entered the early stage of selfishness when it begins to forget God is its resource.

Christ if he is consumed with himself. It doesn't work. This mind-set is dangerous and destroys the body of Christ. A church must use Christ's name, not ours, if it is to be effective in ministering to the world.

> A church must use Christ's name, not ours, if it is to be effective in ministering to the world.

Third, when people use the word *I* more often and start mattering more to themselves, things begin to go their way. Sermons are altered to satisfy their desires, they put people loyal to them and them alone in places of power, services are manipulated for their pleasure, and the church is run like their house instead of God's.

Avoiding the danger zone

These are all early signs of falling prey to selfishness, which will lead to changing the character of God. This is a dangerous way for the church to function. We begin trying to change the character of God when we decide that we are more important than God. The only surefire way to avoid this danger is to remind ourselves every day that we are the created, not the creator. We must saturate ourselves in the Word of God and remember that we were created to glorify the name of Jesus Christ.

Danger Two

Reducing the Depth of Preaching

"I don't need theology. Just give me Jesus." I have heard that statement hundreds of times, and it makes me cringe every time I do. This cry may come from the heart of many people, but it certainly does not come from the heart of God. This statement is anti-biblical and inimical to Christianity. It's like saying, "I want to be saved without knowing the God who saved me." This is man's subtle way of keeping all of the focus on himself. Man would never admit to holding such a position, but if you examine this thought process, you will see that this statement is rooted in a desire to satisfy self.

This dangerous way of thinking has somehow found its way even into our pulpits. Whether through political correctness or man-made religion, it has taken hold. We must understand the danger of letting this happen. It can be summed up in one sentence: as goes the pulpit, so goes the people. How

> As goes the pulpit, so goes the people.

13

do I know this mentality has taken hold? Just watch preachers on television for about ten minutes and you will see it clearly. Most of the messages are totally man-centered. The preachers speak of two subjects: what God can do for us or what we can get from God. There is not much theology or doctrine in this preaching. While such preaching is easy to identify from television preachers, this same mentality can be seen in many churches today. It may not be as visible, but many have succumbed to this type of man-centered preaching.

People love this type of preaching because it is about them. A man-centered gospel makes man happy! A man centered gospel never speaks of Christ yet manages to leave a congregation screaming for more. This is strange to behold. At best, this preaching leads a man to trust in an idea of Christ, but not Christ. At worst, it leads a man to trust in

> A man centered gospel never speaks of Christ yet manages to leave a congregation screaming for more.

himself. I attended services at which a preacher stood up, read a biblical text, closed the Bible, and told stories for thirty minutes. The stories were funny, and he was a great communicator. However, he did not preach the gospel at all. Saddest of all, as the congregation was walking out, someone said to me, "Man, that guy can preach." I wanted to say, "What guy?"

Preaching is saying what God said, not repeating the latest joke traveling across the Internet. We must wise up or our churches will lose their power as we forsake the Word of God to please ourselves. We cannot reduce the depth of our preaching to fit in or be cool. We must preach the whole counsel of God to see life change.

What does the Bible say about preaching?

This is a problem that can destroy a church. If you want concrete evidence, the best place to find it is in God's Word. So what does God say about preaching? If we are going to preach for life change, what does such preaching look like?

First, we need to understand that life change does not begin with us but with God. That is why preaching must start with God, not man's issues. If preaching begins with man's issues, then man will never get to God. He will continually try to use preaching as a springboard to talk about himself.

> If preaching begins with man's issues, then man will never get to God. He will continually try to use preaching as a springboard to talk about himself.

Second, we must realize there is no power in preaching without the Word. To preach without the Word is to do nothing more than tickle ears. Tickling ears has never pardoned anyone of sin. So preaching must be rooted in God and saturated with the Word.

Listen to what Paul tells Timothy in 2 Timothy 4:1–4. "I charge you therefore before God and the Lord Jesus Christ, who will judge the living and the dead at His appearing and His kingdom: Preach the Word! Be ready in season and out of season. Convince, rebuke, exhort, with all long-suffering and teaching. For the time will come when they will not endure sound doctrine, but according to their own desires, because they have itching ears, they will heap up for themselves teachers; and they will turn their ears away from the truth, and be turned aside to fables."

That passage offers an excellent description of what I am saying. Let's examine these verses and the context. Timothy is a young preacher being mentored by the apostle Paul. So Paul begins by saying in effect, "Preach, Timothy. God's watching." That is enough to humble any man who dares stand behind the pulpit, which is why Paul says it. He wants Timothy to remember that besides preaching for God and about God, he is preaching to God. Paul wants to remind him that God will someday make him answer for what he preaches.

Next, Paul tells Timothy to preach only the Word. He does not tell him to preach about the Word or preach around the Word. He says, "Preach the Word!" There are two reasons he tells Timothy this. First, it is always safe to say what God says. The Word of God is His voice to us. Second, only the Word has the power to set us free.

Here Paul gives young Timothy a sense of accountability for his preaching and an idea of what to preach. Paul also clarifies just what the Word can do. We see an exhaustive list of powerful things the Word accomplishes. Finally, Paul shows Timothy the purpose of preaching. Man will turn away from the truth. If man turns from the truth, what hope does he have? Where can he find hope? Nowhere, which is why Paul says it is so important to preach the Word. Only the Word of God will bring man to the truth.

Hebrews 4:12–13 says, "For the word of God is living and powerful, and sharper than any two-edged sword, piercing even to the division of soul and spirit, and of joints and marrow, and is a discerner of the thoughts and intents of the heart. And there is no creature hidden from His sight, but all things are naked and open to the eyes of Him to whom we must give account."

That says it all. The substance of our preaching should be the Word of God because it can get to the very depth of

> Reducing the depth of preaching reduces the desire for God.

who we are and has the power to transform our lives. No pastor should ever reduce the depth of his preaching but should preach the Word thoroughly and passionately.

Reducing the depth of preaching reduces the desire for God. The moment a pastor begins to reduce the depth of his preaching is the moment his people begin to diminish their desire for the knowledge of God. We search the Word of God for only one reason: to see God. All instruction, rebuke, and exhortation flow from that. If Scripture is designed to help us see God and we are not getting Scripture, we are not seeing God. At the least, we are not seeing Him clearly.

A seminary professor once told me, "If people deepened their desire for the Word, it would make their worship more intimate." That is a profound statement. I can see that truth in my marriage. I have been married to Dee Dee for eighteen years, and I am still learning about her. The more I get to know her, the more intimate we become. The same is true with God. The more you spend time in the Word, the more you see Him. The more you see Him, the more you will love Him. The more you love Him, the more you desire to see Him. This is why preachers should just preach the Word! It is the only thing with the power to transform a congregation for the glory of God.

If the Word is so powerful, why would a preacher reduce the depth of his preaching? Why would a preacher choose storytelling over preaching the power found in the Word? What leads a man of God to disregard God's instructions on preaching? I am sure there are many reasons for this dangerous tactic, but I have narrowed them down to two.

Falling prey to the people

The first reason a preacher reduces the depth of his preaching is because he is being led by his people instead of by God. We find an example of this in Exodus 32. Moses left the people in Aaron's hands while he met with God on Mount Sinai. The people became restless because Moses had not returned, and they discussed making false gods out of their jewelry. The people complained to Aaron about Moses being away so long. They asked Aaron to lead them in making a golden calf to worship. Aaron went along with this travesty, and God told Moses to correct the people or He would kill them.

Several things happened in this situation. First, the people lost hope in Moses' return. This led them to have a sinful desire. They presented their desire to a leader, but the leader did not test the plan with God and caved in to their wishes. This is the scenario that you will see every time a pastor falls prey to his people. It is dangerous for the leader to become the follower. However, it happens regularly in the local church.

> It is dangerous for the leader to become the follower.

There are two reasons for this. First, the people are not satisfied with God and begin to look within themselves for satisfaction. God is no longer enough unless He shows up in their preferred style and according to their timing.

The easiest way to get what they want is to bombard the preacher with complaints about the service. At this point, the man of God has a choice. He can be obedient to God or fall prey to his people. Unfortunately, many choose to fall prey.

The second reason is that the preacher makes his popularity more important than the glory of God. I wish this were not true, but it is. Many times a preacher falls prey to the people because he is more concerned about being accepted by them than about following God. This leads a preacher to shy away from preaching the Word of God. It is offensive to the people, so he begins to focus on messages that will be pleasant to his hearers. As soon as he does that, he has become a pawn of his congregants. His messages will be less about God and more about them. He will spend more of his time studying events and people than studying God's Word. Falling prey to people will certainly reduce the depth of preaching.

Falling prey to himself

The second reason a pastor reduces the depth of preaching is because he falls prey to himself. A pastor's worst enemy is himself. If a pastor is not careful, he can fall prey to his own desires. This begins rather subtly, generally with a simple pleasure. The more the pleasure is indulged, the more enjoyable it gets. Before long,

> A pastor's worst enemy is himself.

it is competing against the pastor's calling. If this indulgence is not held in check, the pastor will spend more time on his pleasure than on his calling. This will weaken his ministry and reduce the depth of his preaching—all because the pastor has chosen to play instead of prepare.

When the pastor plays, his ministry will deteriorate in several ways. First, he will begin to rely on his own efforts in stead of relying on God for a fresh word. He will regularly repeat sermons that he has preached in the past. He will do this because he is comfortable with what he has already done and does not have to spend much time preparing. He will also rely on other people's studies, other people's sermons, and re-preach them instead of his own. With the age of the internet, such practices are common in pulpits today. Secondly, the pastor will resort to other types of services to replace his responsibility to prepare a message. The examples here are numerous but let me suggest two common scenarios. One church I know regularly extends the music service allowing the preaching to only be filler to the hymns and choruses. Singing is wonderful and is ordained by God, but it cannot and must not replace the preaching of God's Word. Some churches even replace preaching with testimony services on a regular basis. While I am not against members testifying or testimony services, I am against the pastor using this as a means to circumvent his responsibility. Resting on the gifts of others instead of relying on the gift of preaching is unacceptable and results in the pastor reducing the depth of preaching. A lot of things in worship can accompany the Word, but nothing in worship can replace the Word. All of these things are dangerous for the body of Christ. When this happens, a pastor has weakened his ministry. The only way to strengthen a people is to teach them what God has said about Himself. When the depth of preaching is reduced, it does not please the heart of God or transform people. Unfortunately, this happens every Sunday in a pulpit near you.

Avoiding the danger zone

The depth of preaching is reduced for many reasons, none of them good. The Bible is clear on the necessity of preaching the Word of God. We must remember that the Word is vital in our sanctification process. Without it, how will we know what God has said? Therefore, every pastor must dedicate himself to the study of God's Word. Every pastor should surround himself with men who will hold him accountable for preaching the Word. Every pastor should guard himself by the Word, with the Word, for the sake of the Word.

> A lot of things in worship can accompany the Word, but nothing in worship can replace the Word.

Danger Three

Minimizing the Gospel

What is the gospel? There are many answers to that question even within the body of Christ. Some see the gospel as the part of the sermon where the pastor tells people they must be saved. Many consider the gospel to be obeying the rules of the Bible. Still others believe the gospel is the story of Jesus. But what is the gospel?

The word *gospel* in Greek means "good news." In general, gospel is any good news. However, in Christianity, the gospel is the good news of Jesus. It is the reality that Jesus, God's Son, gave His life on the cross for sinners. The Bible says in 2 Corinthians 5:21, "For He made Him who knew no sin to be sin for us, that we might become the righteousness of God in Him."

However, not only does the gospel exist in the cross, but it existed before the cross. The gospel is not just Jesus dying on the cross; it is Jesus living before the foundations of the world and continuing to live for all eternity. With that hope comes the good news. The gospel is not just about what Jesus did. It is about who He is and who He represents. Certainly the cross is important for us in terms of salvation, but Jesus was important before the cross. The gospel is the whole story of Christ and His redemption of man, from eternity past to eternity future. This story is one of grace, mercy, perfection, and love. This is a good gospel.

> The gospel is the whole story of Christ and His redemption of man, from eternity past to eternity future.

Why is it good?

What makes the gospel so good? The answer lies in its simplicity. The gospel is not good because it is complex, because it is a mystery, or because it is a sweet thought for humans. The gospel is good news because it answers the bad news. In fact, the Bible says it is the only answer to the bad news. This is the point at which people begin to minimize the gospel. Our politically correct society has convinced us that we cannot tell people bad news because that is not nice. The problem with this assertion is that people cannot fully understand the good news until they know the bad news that the good news is meant to address.

> The gospel is good news because it answers the bad news.

So what is this bad news? Here are some verses that offer a clear answer. Romans 5:12 says, "Therefore, just as through one man sin entered the world and death through sin, and thus death spread to all men, because all sinned." This verse offers humanity no comfort. Basically it says we are sinners and will experience death because of this. What does this verse mean by death? We experience three types of death through sin. First, there is physical death, which brings separation from other humans. Second, we experience spiritual death, separation from God through sin. Third, we suffer eternal death, which means we are separated from God for eternity in hell. All of that in just one verse—that is bad news!

There is more bad news. Romans 3:10–18 says, "There is none righteous, no, not one; there is none who understands; there is none who seeks after God. They have all turned aside; they have together become unprofitable; there is none who does good, no, not one. Their throat is an open tomb; with their tongues they have practiced deceit; the poison of asps is under their lips; whose mouth is full of cursing and bitterness. Their feet are swift to shed blood; destruction and misery are in their ways. And the way of peace they have not known. There is no fear of God in their eyes."

It is hard to find anything in these verses that would leave us pleased with ourselves. This passage says we are bad people who practice evil, hurt others, and have no respect for God. Ouch! This is one of those verses that cut straight to the heart. Some of you reading it do not believe that you are what this verse says. You do not like to hear anyone say that you are bad. After all, you can think of dozens of people who are worse than you.

A preacher friend told a story about a woman who came down the aisle to get saved. He explained what salvation is about and asked her to pray and admit that she was a sinner unworthy to be saved. To his surprise, she said, "I am not going to say

> A minimized gospel may contain the cross, but not the reason for the cross. It is the reason for the cross, not the cross itself, that offends the depraved man.

that. I am not unworthy to be saved." He responded, "Miss, you can sit back down." He did that because he understood that a person must realize the bad news to understand the good news. But many people do not like the fact that they are sinners who are not good enough to be saved.

The temptation to minimize the gospel springs from this mind-set. A familiar saying advises, "If it feels good, do it." A companion adage says, "If it hurts, don't do it." That is the philosophy that some preachers live by. They do not want to say anything to offend the hearer. This leads to minimizing the gospel. A minimized gospel may contain the cross, but not the reason for the cross. It is the reason for the cross, not the cross itself, that offends the depraved man. To refuse to speak of the reason for the gospel is to refuse to speak of the power of the gospel. The power of the gospel is that it takes bad men and reconciles them to God. So the good news and the bad news are both part of the gospel. They are welded together just as faith and works. Good news is always good because bad news is always bad.

Dangers of minimizing the gospel

Minimizing the gospel has many dangerous repercussions, all of which can and will do great harm to the body of Christ. First, minimizing the gospel reduces the glory of Christ. If we do not speak of how sinful and disobedient man is, then we cannot understand just how amazing the grace of Jesus is.

The apostle Paul teaches us how amazing the grace of God is by showing us how bad man is. Romans 5:6–8 says, "For when we were still without strength, in due time Christ came and died for the ungodly. For scarcely for a righteous man would one die; yet perhaps for a good man someone would even dare to die. But God demonstrated His love toward us, in that while we were sinners, Christ died for the ungodly."

Paul makes it abundantly clear that Jesus died for ungodly sinners. He also shows us the miraculous extent of God's grace. In verse 7, he notes that it is rare for someone to die for a good man. So if people rarely die for good men, it is unheard of that they should die for bad men. Paul then tells us that

God showed us how much He loved us by sending His Son to die for bad people. Wow! How amazing is that?

When you minimize the gospel, not only do you ignore Scripture, but you change the story line, which would then read something like this. All people are good and do not need a savior, but Jesus died for them anyway. How nice of Jesus to do that.

That story line is missing something and reduces the love of God. It is not amazing grace if we do not need it. So to fail to speak of sin because doing so is deemed offensive or negative is to diminish the glory of Christ and His work on the cross. That is dangerous for any body of Christ.

> It is not amazing grace if we do not need it.

Second, minimizing the gospel leads to a me-driven church. When people choose not to speak of sin because they consider this negative, they quickly begin to exalt themselves to fend off the thought of being sinners. This leads to sermons that speak only of how amazing we are and how God has a wonderful plan for our lives. Man begins to focus on man and not on the gospel. The gospel becomes a tool for man to exalt himself. The preacher begins to choose Scripture passages that speak of what God can do for man. This leads man to worship God's gifts and blessings instead of God Himself. Sermons are man-centered and not God-centered. Genuine worship is not found, because man never gets past himself.

In a recent sermon, I said that worship always begins and ends with God. First we recognize God for who He is. Then we see ourselves for who we are, sinners in need of mercy and grace. When we see ourselves for who we are that points us back to God. For any man to truly worship, he must follow that pattern. This pattern of worship can be found in Isaiah 6:1–9. Isaiah says in verse 1 that he saw the Lord seated on His throne, high and lifted up. In verse 5, Isaiah says he saw that he was undone and a man of unclean lips. He goes as far as confessing everyone else's sin, saying all those around him were unclean. Then in verse 8 he hears the Lord ask, "Whom shall I send?"

This is a perfect picture of a God-centered worship service. Isaiah started and ended with God. This is the way worship is supposed to be. But what if a man does not want to see himself as bad? How would his worship service go? The Bible gives us an example. Luke 18:9–14 tells the story of two men—a tax collector and a Pharisee. The Pharisee starts his worship with God, but does not see himself for who he is. This leads him to boast in himself and not in God. The tax collector, however, starts with God, sees himself for who he is, and ends with worship of God. Therefore, verse 14 says, the tax collector was the one justified.

When man minimizes the gospel by leaving out the bad

news, he begins to think highly of himself and travels down a slippery slope toward making himself his own god. Man cannot worship the Savior correctly if he refuses to see himself correctly. That is why it is so important to preach the whole counsel of God within the body of Christ. Yes, it may hurt to be cut by the Word of God, but it is necessary for our sanctification. It is necessary for us to receive the gospel in its entirety. If we don't, our worship service will be shallow and man-centered, leaving us in the sin of pride.

Avoiding the danger zone

The only way we can keep from minimizing the gospel is to keep the gospel at the center of everything. The gospel of Jesus is in every page of the Bible. We need to read it, study it, and live it. We should always remind ourselves that we did not deserve this glorious salvation that we received. It is a gift from almighty God. Our worship should always begin with God and end with God. We must remember that we are king's kids, but not by our own doing. If we do this, we will never minimize the gospel for our own satisfaction.

Danger Four

CHOOSING POOR LEADERSHIP

This past summer I was invited to preach at an all-boys camp in Louisiana. The boys ranged in age from seven to twelve. If you have never had the opportunity to preach at one of these camps, you are missing out on some curious phenomena. Many of the boys can go all week without bathing. Some even wear the same underwear for a solid week. It was an interesting and eventful week.

One of the most interesting moments came when I was teaching a breakout session after Bible study. I assigned the group to take building blocks and put together a tower as high as they could make it. Then they had to transfer the tower from our room onto a stage. This task seemed easy. The catch was to see if they could follow directions and work together. As the boys gathered in the room, I gave them instructions and chose a leader for the group. Two groups carried out this task that day. It was interesting to see how they managed.

This activity may have seemed unimportant, but it taught me a lot about choosing leaders. The first leader was arrogant and full of himself. He chose his best buddy to assist him on the project. The instructions were that everyone had to put at least four pieces on the tower, but he and his friend would let hardly anyone else touch it. They pushed everyone away because they thought that their idea was best and that everyone else would mess up their tower.

The second leader was timid and quiet. He did basically the opposite of the other leader. He started building and did not say much to the others about what to do, so they just grabbed blocks and started building on their own. So we had about three towers being built at one time, hardly what was needed to get the task accomplished. Both leaders eventually got towers built and onto the stage. Of course adults had to step in and make sure they got the job done. Had it not been for the adults, the leaders would never have succeeded.

So what does this story teach us about leadership? First, it shows us that leadership is central to getting things accomplished. Second, it shows us that bad leadership can work against the desired goal. I wish I could say that the plague of bad leadership is confined to children's games, but I would be lying. Let us examine the danger of bad leadership, the importance of proper biblical leadership, and how to avoid bad leadership.

The danger of bad leadership

The most important thing to remember about leadership is that leaders are leading other people. They are not casually producing ideas and trying them out on no one. They are sharing their central beliefs with others in hopes that they will follow. Every leader is leading someone somewhere. Most people would agree that we need leaders in all areas of life. We need leaders in our churches just as much as we need them at an all-boys camp. The danger is not found in the fact that we need leaders; the danger is found in choosing the wrong leaders. If we choose the wrong leaders, we could end up destroying the local church and the influence it has in our communities. That is the last thing we need in this culture. The church must be an active, light-bearing, stable witness to our culture.

> The danger is not found in the fact that we need leaders; the danger is found in choosing the wrong leaders.

Bad leadership can do several things to destroy the church. The first danger in choosing the wrong leader is obvious. He will lead in the wrong direction. My son summed up that thought after a sermon I once preached. He said, "You can lead only in the direction you are going." That sounds simple, but this is a complex issue. That's because there are many reasons for choosing wrong leadership.

The most common reason is desperation. When a church gets desperate for a leader, it sometimes moves ahead of God and chooses the wrong man. It is almost as if the church has decided that it will take what it can get instead of choosing God's man. When this happens, the leader will end up taking the church in the wrong direction. This happens not because the leader is defiant or manipulative but because where he is going is not where the church needs to go.

I know of a church that hired a pastor that it thought was the right man for the job. He proved not to be the right man at all. This was a small country church whose members thought that caring for the community was vital. It is! The pastor thought that the church had to be run more like a business. He therefore took a more hands-off approach by spending little time in the community, living away from the church, and running it as if it were a mega church. He was leading in a direction that church members did not want to go. His tenure did not last long.

A church also makes a mistake when it chooses a leader with a gift other than the one it requires. The Bible is very clear in 1 Corinthians 12:4–5 that there are many gifts. Paul says, "There are diversities of gifts, but the same spirit. There are different ministries, but the same Lord." He then mentions these gifts, explaining that believers are called to use certain gifts in certain areas.

Many churches fail in this area of leadership. They choose pastors based on the gifts they like most. Some members are drawn to evangelistic ministries, some to teaching ministries, some to healing ministries, some to administration. Because they are blinded by their own gifts, they may choose a candidate who is not the right man for the task at hand. For example, evangelists and pastors are separate types of preachers. The evangelist is usually more fiery and energetic because he has an urgent message of salvation that he feels must be declared every day. The pastor is generally more polished and careful in his approach because he understands that his purpose is to equip the saints for the work of the ministry. He realizes that this is an ongoing process and that he shouldn't expect an immediate response. However, many churches search for evangelists to pastor their congregations. As much as I like fiery preaching, I believe that this is a grave mistake that can take a toll on a church in the long run. The reason is simple: the evangelist is not called to pastor. He is called to introduce people to the gospel.

Generally, when an evangelist is chosen to pastor, a church will see numerical growth, but over time it will not grow as much spiritually. That's because the evangelist has one message: get saved. This is the most important message of all, and every pastor must preach it. However, the man who is saved must grow spiritually. Therefore he needs to learn what God says in His Word about being equipped.

This problem comes from a misunderstanding of what the gathering of believers is about. The gathering has never been about the lost; the going is. The gathering is meant to equip the saints that they might go and win the lost. Many churches choose leaders based on an improper emphasis on gifts. This problem is just as dangerous as the first, since people are again led in the wrong direction. The wrong leader keeps them in spiritual infancy instead of guiding them to spiritual maturity. Having the right leader in the wrong place is just as bad as having no leader at all.

The second danger in choosing the wrong leadership is that it breeds more bad leadership. In Matthew 15:14, Jesus said, "Let them alone. They are blind leading the blind. And if the blind leads the blind, they will both fall into a ditch." The truth of this statement is clear. As my son said, "You can lead only in the direction you are going." Leaders will always place in leadership those who think like them. It is important for other leaders to be headed the same way. This brings continuity to leadership. But a problem arises when you have the wrong leader. He will choose other leaders who are headed in the wrong direction to lead others the same way. This process breeds a dangerous cycle within the body of Christ. Bad leaders produce bad followers. Eventually they all fall into a ditch.

No matter how it happens, choosing the wrong leadership weakens the body of Christ. Most of the time it is done unintentionally and without thought. Nonetheless, the wrong choice can cause serious harm to the witness of the church. It can cost the church its influence in the community. It can be so damaging that it takes years for the church to regain the community's respect. The last thing we need is for churches to be silent in our communities. It is crucial that we choose the right leaders and ensure that they serve in the areas suited for their gifts. When we do this, we maximize our potential for changing our communities for the sake of Christ.

Biblical leadership

What does God say about leadership? What qualifications does He establish for leaders? Let's examine a passage on choosing the right leaders. Acts 6 recounts how the early church chose its first deacons. Some believers felt that widows were being neglected in the daily distribution of food, so they complained to the apostles. The apostles realized that their primary responsibility was to teach the Word of God, not get bogged down in service to widows, so they instructed the people to choose from among themselves men who could serve in this area. The disciples gave advice on how to select these leaders. In Acts 6:3, they said, "Therefore, brethren, seek out from among you seven men of good reputation, full of the Holy Spirit and wisdom, whom you may appoint over this business."

This passage offers criteria for choosing leaders. First, the apostles said to "choose from among yourselves." This standard is crucial when considering men who are to be of service to the people. If a man lives among them, he will know their needs. It would be very hard for a man to serve a community in which he does not live.

Second, they wanted "men of good reputation." That is a no-brainer. If you are going to choose men to serve a large number of people, you shouldn't have to worry about their actions. They must be men whom people respect, men of humility, men who know how to handle people. The last thing the apostles wanted was more problems. Therefore, they instructed believers to make sure they chose leaders who were upstanding among the people.

> It would be very hard for a man to serve a community in which he does not live.

Third, they said leaders should be "full of the Holy Spirit." This is probably the most important qualification. This is vital because men full of the Spirit will be led by God to lead people where God wants them to go. Men full of the Spirit will be constrained by the Spirit to practice love, joy, patience, kindness, mercy, goodness, and self-control, qualities needed to deal with people correctly.

Finally, the apostles pointed to wisdom. They knew that a man needed wisdom to solve problems. They were not just talking about godly wisdom, but practical wisdom. If you choose people without wisdom to be problem solvers, they will always be problem solvers because they will continue to cause problems.

You can see from this moment in early church history exactly what the apostles thought about choosing leaders. It would be great if the local church today chose deacons this way. Instead leadership often falls to men who are as unqualified as a barstool. This is one reason our churches are in the condition they are in. We have leaders who do not lead because they are not leaders. We've got men who are more concerned about the titles attached to their names than the service that is supposed to accompany these titles. As long as we continue to place people in leadership by default, we will continue to be led in the wrong direction. One thing is for sure: leaders will lead only in the direction they are going.

> If you choose people without wisdom to be problem solvers, they will always be problem solvers because they will continue to cause problems.

Avoiding the danger zone

How can we avoid placing the wrong people in leadership? First, we should be led by the Spirit, not the desire to fill a spot. Second, we should evaluate potential leaders according to biblical parameters and choose them according to the Word, not a popularity contest. Third, we must avoid putting leaders in positions that do not require the gifts that God has given them. If we will do these things, we will maximize our leaders' strengths and will take the church in the right direction.

Danger Five

STEALING THE GREAT COMMISSION

Several years ago, I received a call from the mechanic who was working on my motor home. He told me that my bus had been broken into over the weekend. Arriving at the mechanic's shop to assess the situation, I could definitely tell the bus had been burgled. There was shattered glass all over the parking lot, the driver's seat, and the floorboard. The evidence was overwhelming. I wanted to see what had been stolen. I frantically searched every inch of the motor home, but the only thing I could find missing was my video camera. I was thankful that nothing else had been taken, but I was upset that someone had broken into my motor home and stolen my camera.

I still remember entering my motor home and finding overwhelming evidence that someone had stolen my camera. This brings to mind the fifth danger to the church: stealing the Great Commission. As I enter America's churches, the evidence is overwhelming that someone has stolen the Great Commission from most of them. We seem to have more buildings and more money than ever, but our people are more biblically illiterate than they were fifty years ago.

Why do our churches seem so weak? Jesus said in Matthew 16:18, "And I say to you that you are Peter and on this rock I will build my church, and the gates of hell shall not prevail against it." If that is true, why does the church seem so powerless? Why are many of our churches not baptizing or growing in the grace and knowledge of Jesus? The answer lies in the state of the Great Commission.

The command of Christ

Jesus spent the last three years of His life walking this earth with twelve men, teaching them how to follow Him. He lodged with them, ate with them, and served them. He modeled what Christianity is supposed to look like. After His death and resurrection, Jesus was getting ready to ascend into heaven and prepare a place for us. Before He did, He left His followers with one last command. Jesus said, "All authority in heaven and earth has been given to me. Go therefore and make disciples of all nations, baptizing them in the name of the Father and of the Son and of the Holy Spirit, teaching them to observe all things that I have commanded you; and lo, I am with you always, even to the end of age."

Jesus asked His followers to go and make more followers.

This is what we call the Great Commission. Think of all the commands He could have given. He could have said, "Hunger and thirst for righteousness," "Lay up treasure in heaven," or "Don't forget to be salt and light." Instead He said, "Go and make disciples." Why? What makes this command so special? This command is special because Jesus knew the state of His kingdom on earth depended upon it. Because this command is so important, we need to see what it means, who has stolen it, and the danger in its removal.

The first thing we must notice is that Jesus said He has all authority. What does that mean? Albert Barnes puts it this way:

> The son of God as creator had an original right to all things, to control them and to dispose of them. But the universe is put under him more particularly as mediator, that he might redeem his people; that he might gather a church; that he might defend his chosen; that he might subdue all their enemies, and bring them off as conquerors and more than conquerors. It is in reference to this, doubtless, that he speaks here of power or authority committed to him over all things, that he might redeem, defend and save the church he purchased with his own blood. His mediatorial government extends, therefore, over the material world, over angels, or devils, or wicked men, and his own people.

43

— Albert Barnes, *Barnes' Notes on the New Testament* (Grand Rapids, Michigan: Kregel Publications, 1980)

To explain this in simpler terms, I will paraphrase Barnes. Jesus reigns over all things in this complex world. But Jesus wasn't simply declaring Himself to be all-powerful. He wanted His disciples to understand that if they were going at His request, they had nothing to fear because the One sending them was king over all. To walk in the authority of Christ is to walk as an extension of Christ.

Jesus wanted His disciples to go with that authority. He didn't mean that they should plan a Tuesday night visitation each week

> Every disciple in Scripture was made while someone was going somewhere.

and invite people to attend church. There is nothing wrong with that, but it wasn't what Jesus meant. He intended that His disciples should, in fact, go. This going doesn't involve a specific time, but a lifestyle. The idea is that as we go on with life we are to be making disciples. The life of Jesus Himself makes this clear. He was constantly on the move but made disciples everywhere He went. He made them in the fields, in the synagogues, on the lake, and even in the tombs. Every disciple in Scripture was made while someone was going somewhere. Here are a few examples.

- The deaf mute, whom Jesus encountered after He left Tyre-Sidon and came to Decapolis (Mark 7:31–32).

- Philip and Nathaniel, whom Jesus met as He was going to Galilee (John 1:43–45).

- Peter and Andrew, whom Jesus found as He walked by the Sea of Galilee (Matt. 4:18).

- Matthew, whom Jesus saw at a booth after healing a paralytic (Matt. 9:9).

- A demon-possessed man, whom Jesus met after going from one side of the lake to the other (Mark 5:1–2).

Jesus never set a day aside to make disciples. He did it as He was going from place to place. As we go about our day, doing whatever we are doing, we also are to be making disciples. Christ commands that we be about the Father's business. Jesus delivered this message in Luke 2:41–49 when His parents left Him behind. After a day of travel, they realized Jesus was not with them or other family members. Returning to Jerusalem, they found Jesus at the temple, teaching men. When His frantic mother questioned what He was doing, He said, "I must be about my Father's business." If this agenda is right for the Son of God, it is right for us. The command is clear. We must make disciples by the authority of Christ.

We are to be making disciples not just on Sunday but as we live life. To be effective at this task, we must understand what is meant by *disciple*. A disciple is simply a learner.

There are two steps to becoming a disciple of Christ. The first is coming to faith in Jesus Christ as Lord. The second happens after salvation when a person can understand spiritual things and begins to learn from a teacher the ways of Christ.

To make disciples, we must lead people to Christ and teach them His ways. To teach Christ's ways, we must do two things. First, we have to study these ways through prayer, the Bible, and intimacy with Him. Second, we must teach others what

> We imitate to duplicate.

we have learned. This is what Jesus did for His disciples. He spent three years with them, then sent them out into the world to do as He did. Paul did the same thing. In 1 Corinthians 11:1, he says, "Imitate me as I imitate Christ." That is the formula in a nutshell! Paul puts it so elegantly but so simply. Do what I do, he says, because I am doing what Jesus did. The principle of discipleship is summed up in one phrase: we imitate to duplicate.

The thief among us

If this Great Commission is so important to Jesus and His kingdom, why is it absent from many of our churches? Why are the seats empty and our churches dead? It is because someone has broken into the church and stolen the Great Commission. Who would do such a thing? None other than the church itself. It turns out that those who were commanded to go have sat down and stayed. How has the church stolen what was given to it? The simplest answer is that we have removed the commission from the Great Commission. We have taken the command of Christ and decided we know a better way. We have put the fingerprint of man over the blueprint of God. We have done several things to put man's signature on God's idea.

Seeker-friendly movements

Somehow we have decided that the lost man cannot handle the language of the Bible. Therefore we have chosen to befriend him at the expense of the Word of God. We have developed a movement to keep the lost man at ease. This movement advocates changing the language of the preacher and the surroundings of the church to make the lost man comfortable there.

The danger of doing this is that we have developed a system that God did not design or encourage. The idea is not to get the lost to enter and be comfortable. That would rule out preaching anything convicting. If that is the case, we must ask the Spirit to leave, because one of His functions is to convict. That leaves us with a watered-down version of the gospel and a church service where the Spirit is quenched. This is not biblical and is contrary to what Christ commanded.

This movement causes us to be comfortable as well. We think if we make the church as appealing as possible for the lost, they will come without us ever having to go to them. This is a dangerous combination! The idea of the Great Commission is for us to go out into a sinful world and present the love of Christ, not to change everything we do to make people come to us and be comfortable.

Program-driven

Another popular escape route from the Great Commission is to create massive programs that draw people to the church. Once again, this is dangerous. Programs can be very effective in sharing the love of Christ, but they can also be very effective in keeping us from the Great Commission.

While I was pastoring my first church, God began to move every Sunday during the services. We were experiencing a revival. It was very exciting to come to church, because no one knew what God would do next. In the midst of all this, one church member came to me and said, "We need to do forty days of purpose." I responded, "What for? God is saving people nearly every Sunday." I think we will just keep doing the same thing we have been doing."

> Programs can be very effective in sharing the love of Christ, but they can also be very effective in keeping us from the Great Commission.

For some reason, people have decided that programs are

where it's at. When a program becomes your go-to option, your go-to option has gone wrong. We are putting more emphasis on programs than on telling people about Jesus. The witnessing statement most often used by Christians today is "We want to invite you to our church." That's because our philosophy has changed. We just want to get people to church so they can see all the good programs we offer. Surely this will get them hooked on our church, we believe.

We are going overboard trying to get the lost to come to our churches. We are using any means, from changing services to being friendlier to building massive programs. The problem is that the gathering has never been about the lost; the going is. The whole point of gathering as believers is to become equipped to go out and engage the lost with the gospel. Certainly lost people come to our services. Certainly we can invite people to our churches. But if we replace the Great Commission with those things, we have sinned against God. These programs and movements change every few years because they are not God's plan for spreading the gospel. We are!

> the gathering has never been about the lost; the going is.

Dangers of replacing the Great Commission

These approaches are dangerous to the existence of our churches for six reasons. First, they are disobedient to

Christ's command. It is clear that Jesus never intended for us to sit around and devise ways to get lost people to come to us. He specifically said, "Go." Second, these methods can spawn complacency in the body. If we are consistently allowing programs and movements to do the work for us, we risk getting lazy. What's the point of doing anything if we have a well-oiled machine to do it for us? That is what happens when we become dependent on programs.

Third, these programs and movements bring about a lack of compassion. When a church is program-driven, the people forget about those who do not participate. The lady down the street who needs to be shown the love of Christ does not get to see it if she does not attend church. Those most important to us are those who take part in our programs. These people receive all of our compassion, while others receive our ridicule because they are absent from our programs.

Fourth, these movements and programs weaken the church. People who work in the programs become dependent on the programs and involvement in them. This causes them to abandon the Great Commission and cling to the programs. This weakens the body of Christ. To grow in Christ, people must be obedient to His commands. They must be actively going.

The fifth reason this trend is dangerous is that it breeds immaturity within the body. The seeker-friendly movement vows to keep everything at a surface level. You cannot go too deep because you may offend or confuse someone who is lost. This creates an atmosphere of immaturity. Coupling immature Christians with programs is a disaster waiting to happen.

Finally, reliance on programs sets in motion a cycle of methods that end up killing discipleship. A well-oiled program will draw people to a church at first. However, when the program gets old or another church comes up with a better one, what will church leaders do? They will call a committee meeting and tell members to brainstorm about a new program. This vicious cycle is being repeated in many of our churches. Is it because we want to save lost people, or is it because we have stolen the Great Commission? I am convinced it is because we have decided that our way is better than God's way.

God has given us the guidelines. Jesus said He died to build a church, and He gave us the strategies and techniques to assist Him. We simply need to follow them. Program-driven methods are a dangerous way to facilitate a church body. If we want the church to be powerful again, we must go and make disciples. The key to effective evangelism is effective discipleship. Let's return the Great Commission to the church.

Avoiding the Danger Zone

Avoiding the danger of stealing the Great Commission all begins with you. Take a moment to evaluate why you do not participate in the Great Commission. There are several reasons people fail to take part. See which, if any, apply to you.

First, most people do not participate because it is easier to get people to come to them. Second, people do not fulfill the Great Commission out of fear. They are afraid that people's unbelief is stronger than their belief. Finally, many shirk the Great Commission because they are unconcerned about the souls of men. If you have ignored Christ's command to make disciples, repent. Turn your heart toward Jesus and remind yourself that He purchased you with His blood. Remember how good He has been to you and go tell the world. My friend Tory DarDar said it like this, "What you love the most about God let others love that about you." Love to tell the story of Jesus and His love.

Regaining Perspective

If you consider all of the dangers we have mentioned, you will find one common denominator in them: the love of self. It shows up everywhere. It is found in our homes, jobs, classrooms, play places, and even our pulpits. This love for ourselves creeps in unnoticed by many but is exploited by all. It is a dangerous ploy that the enemy uses to stifle the work of the church. We must come to our senses and stop playing these games at the foot of the cross.

The more we reign in our churches, the more our churches begin to look like us. The more our churches look like us, the more they

> The more our churches look like us, the more they fade into the world.

fade into the world. The watchman must sound the alarm to warn the people that the enemy cometh. Will you do what it takes to get our churches back on track? Will you take the steps needed to renew the submission of our churches to Christ? What are the steps that we need to take?

Proper perspective

One of the greatest worship scenes in the Bible is found in the sixth chapter of the book of Isaiah. All of us must have this worship experience to restore things to their rightful place. An Isaiah moment would help make our churches the churches that Jesus died to create. We need a moment when we see the glory of the Almighty, the shame of man, and the commission to go. Let's see what the prophet saw. Isaiah 6:1–8 says,

> In the year king Uzziah died, I saw the Lord high and lifted up, and the train of His robe filled the temple. Above it stood seraphim; each one had six wings: with two he covered his face, with two he covered his feet, and with two he flew. And one cried to another and said: "Holy, holy, holy is the Lord of hosts; the whole earth is filled with His glory!" And the doorposts were shaken by the voice of him who cried out, and the house was filled with smoke. So I said: "Woe is me, for I am undone! I am a man of unclean lips in the midst of a people of unclean lips; for my eyes have seen the King, the Lord of Hosts." Then one of the seraphim flew to me, having in his hand a live coal which he had taken with the tongs from the altar. And he

touched my mouth with it and said: "Behold, this has touched your lips; your iniquity is taken away, and your sin purged." Also I heard the voice of the Lord saying: "Whom shall I send, and who will go for Us?" Then I said, here am I! Send me."

God reveals three perspectives to Isaiah in this passage. These perspectives in turn reveal the things we must do to make our churches what God created them to be. Let's take them one at a time.

Glory of God

In his vision, Isaiah sees some amazing things. First, he sees the throne of the Lord Jesus lifted up in all of its glory. Then he sees angelic beings singing of God's greatness. Finally, he sees the splendor of the King. Every part of this vision declares something magnificent about God. The establishment of this throne declares the authority of Jesus. The seraphim singing His praises testify to His glory, while the angel sent to touch Isaiah's tongue with a coal is a sign of God's grace.

One part of the passage goes even deeper to explain Christ's glory and authority. In verse 1, Isaiah mentions the train of His robe filling the temple. Why would Isaiah discuss what Jesus was wearing? This information is important because it underscores Christ's glory. Robes were a sign of royalty and prestige, of social and religious rank. Therefore, Isaiah is being reminded of the royalty of Christ.

Isaiah goes even deeper by describing the length of the robe. History teaches us that when a king went into battle and defeated another king, he would cut the corner of the robe as a sign of victory over that king. Many times a king would take the corner of the robe of a defeated king and sew it onto his own robe. This would make the train of the robe longer. The more successful a king was in battle, the longer and more colorful the robe. Isaiah sees a king with a robe that fills a whole temple, a king seated on a throne higher than all other thrones. He sees a king who has defeated all other kings of the world. The robe speaks of the very name of God. He is the almighty King of Kings.

In this description, we see how to begin restoring the church. The first step is to see God for who He is. We have diluted the name of God by becoming man-centered

> Heaven is not a democratic society. Just ask Satan.

instead of God- centered. We have to be reminded that He is on His throne and no one can dethrone Him. Heaven is not a democratic society. Just ask Satan. He tried to vote God out of heaven by force and did not succeed. The result will be the same for us if we cling to a man-centered view of God. God is the King of Kings and Lord of Lords.

Shame of man

Once we regain a proper perspective on this God we serve, we will regain a proper perspective on who we are. Once Isaiah sees the Lord God in His proper place, he puts himself in the proper place. Isaiah does this by confessing that he is a sinful man and that his mouth is unclean. He goes a step further, confessing everyone else's sins.

That is not what you are looking for in your friends. It seems mean-spirited of Isaiah to be doing this. However, if you look deeper, you will see his purpose. First, he is not saying anything that the Lord does not already know. Second, he is not pointing to anyone in particular. His purpose in saying this is simply to confess the holiness of God and the sinfulness of man. Isaiah is only speaking the truth. God is holy and man is sinful, and our churches will never be right if this is not a fundamental teaching.

The great thing about this vision is the reminder that God does not have to give us a list of our sins to put us in our place. The only thing He has to do is let us see Him. Being in the presence of God and seeing His holiness will give us a proper perspective on who we are.

Commission to go

After Isaiah regains a proper perspective on God and himself, he is given two great luxuries. The first is forgiveness. God sends a seraphim to touch Isaiah's tongue with a live coal. This is a sign of forgiveness from the Lord Himself. Isaiah, a sinful man, is given the opportunity to be in God's presence and yet walk away forgiven. Second, Isaiah is commissioned by the Lord. The Lord asks, "Who will go for Us?" Isaiah has been in God's presence and has received forgiveness. How could he not volunteer? His response is simply "Send me." Isaiah has seen enough of God that he knows he must obey Him. He knows this not because he sees God as tyrannical or evil but because he recognizes God as a righteous, holy king.

Many people in our churches have decided that they are more important than God. Whether they are minimizing the gospel or choosing poor leadership, it is evident that many churches are run in a sinful way. Too many churches reflect selfish leadership to deny this argument. Too many congregants bear the marks of the world to dismiss the claim.

So what do we do? Let us stand in the presence of the Lord and see Him for who He is, and He will handle the rest. He will cause us to understand our sin, seek forgiveness, receive it, and beg to go. So many people are looking for seven-step programs to solve the problem when all that is needed is to spend seven

> So many people are looking for seven-step programs to solve the problem when all that is needed is to spend seven seconds in God's presence.

seconds in God's presence. It is clear that many churches are falling from within. The greatest question is will they recognize it? God has a glorious purpose for his church. He died to make her holy and powerful. It is up to us to reflect the light of Christ as we do His work on this side of heaven. We must recognize the dangers and do whatever it takes to eliminate them. It is my prayer for every pastor, every deacon, every Christian that we would repent of these dangers and seek the face of God.

Daily Devotions

The Bible says for us to meditate on the Word of God. On the following pages you will find ten days worth of daily devotions that will help you initiate a closer walk with Christ. The greatest part of being a child of God is beaing able to talk with Him daily. I encourage you to drink deeply from the well of truth found in God's Word.

Day One: To know Him

Every so often I receive an XMA newsletter from brother Randy Pierce. XMA is a mission organization based in my home area. Every time I read an issue, one thing stands out the most. It's the group's slogan, "To know him and to make him known." That sums up life for me.

The apostle Paul felt the same way about his life. In Philippians 3:10, he wrote, "My goal is to know Him and the power of His resurrection and the fellowship of His sufferings, being conformed to His death, assuming that I will somehow reach the resurrection from among the dead."

The interesting thing about this verse is that he wrote it around twenty-six years after his salvation experience on the road to Damascus. He wrote this verse about fifteen years after he wrote Galatians 2:20 in which he says, "I have been crucified with Christ and I no longer live, but Christ lives in me. The life I live in the body, I live by faith in the Son of God, who loved me and gave Himself for me."

Doesn't that sound like a man who already knew Christ extremely well? What did he mean, then, when he wrote that his goal was to know Him? Paul had already suffered terrible beatings and other harsh abuses for Christ. Paul knew that sacrifice brings intimacy! He simply meant that even though he was already saved and suffering for Jesus, he wanted to know Christ even more than he did the day before. His life was about intimately knowing Christ each day.

Have you come to that place in your life? Salvation is not the end; it's the beginning. So make up your mind that you will get to know Christ even more today than you did yesterday. Remember that it all begins with God's holy Word. Pray and ask God to help you discover the great truth in His Word and the great joy of knowing Him more.

Notes

Day Two: Take up your cross

"Then he said to [them] all, 'If anyone wants to follow Me, he must deny himself, take up his cross daily and follow Me'" (Luke 9:23 Holman CSB).

This passage of Scripture comes directly after the Lord asks the disciples who people were saying He was. Peter explicitly identifies Him as God's chosen one, the Messiah. After affirming that great truth, Christ gives the disciples a specific outline of what a true follower looks like. He begins by saying, "If anyone desires to follow." Christ makes it clear that everyone has an option. Ethnic background and material status don't matter. All can come. There are no restrictions on who can come.

However, the Lord gives a clear explanation of how a true follower must come. First and foremost, he must deny himself. That means he must disregard his own interests. Life can no longer be about him. Second, the follower must take up his cross. Crucifixion was the most barbaric way anyone could suffer death. No one wanted to carry a cross to the place of execution. To perform that great task, a person had to be under someone's authority. Christ puts it plainly. If you are going to follow Him, you must submit to His authority, and not once at an altar, but every day. That doesn't mean you must get saved every day. It simply means after you've yielded to Him, you must struggle every day to stay submitted to Him. You must choose to give Him authority in your life.

Finally, Christ says, "Follow me." He made that requirement last for a good reason. Jesus knew that if a man couldn't deny himself and submit to His authority, he would never follow Him. This passage has two implications. Nonbelievers can profit by heeding these instructions and following Christ by repenting of their sins and yielding themselves to Him as their Savior and Lord. Believers, who have already repented and declared Him Savior and Lord, should remember that they must continue denying themselves and submitting to His authority every day to be what God wants them to be.

Pray that God will help you through the power of His Word and the leadership of His Holy Spirit to deny yourself, submit to Him daily, and follow His lead.

NOTES

Day Three: Reconciliation

"Now everything is from God, who reconciled us to Himself through Christ and gave us the ministry of reconciliation: that is, in Christ, God was reconciling the world to Himself, not counting their trespasses against them, and He has committed the message of reconciliation to us. Therefore, we are ambassadors for Christ; certain that God is appealing through us, we plead on Christ's behalf, 'Be reconciled to God'" (2 Cor. 5:18–20 Holman CSB).

Someone once gave a great definition of *reconciliation*. It means that something that should have been together all along, but was separated, has been brought back together.

That is such a beautiful picture of our lives as Christians. In the days of Adam and Eve, man gave way to sin, and God's wonderful creation has suffered because of it. Man was separated from his creator. However, God sacrificed His only Son to reconcile sinful mankind to Himself. He returned us to our rightful place, fellowship with Him. Isn't that something special and awesome? What a message!

This verse says that Christ has redeemed us. Not only that, but He has placed us in a position to share that message with others and watch them be reconciled. He says we are His ambassadors. Christ assigned us this task because He had finished His work on earth and returned to the Father, sending the Holy Spirit and interceding on our behalf. Therefore He left us in charge of the gospel message.

An ambassador is a spokesperson for someone in high authority. He speaks with the authority of the person he represents, because the figure of authority sends the message. So it's imperative that we present God's message boldly and unashamedly. After all, we are speaking for the highest authority, Christ Jesus. God has entrusted us with the message and has told us to plead with others to accept that message. *Plead* means to encourage, to appeal. A plea is intended to produce a response. We cannot dictate or manipulate that response, but we are obliged to present the message and let God's Holy Spirit take the message of the gospel and reconcile others to the Father. Remember that you are an ambassador, a spokesperson for the King of Kings.

Pray and thank God for reconciling you to Himself through the blood of Jesus. Ask Him to help you remember that you are His ambassador. Ask Him to remind you to share His message of reconciliation with those around you.

NOTES

Day Four: Propitiation

"He Himself is the propitiation for our sins, and not only for ours, but also for those of the whole world" (1 John 2:2 Holman CSB).

Ultimately, we all get what we deserve. After all, Scripture says a man reaps what he sows. Think of this truth. The God of this universe is so perfect, righteous, and holy that He cannot allow sin in His presence. In fact, He is such a just God that He has no choice but to punish sin. That appears to contradict the loving nature of the God we read about in Scripture. The Bible says He is a forgiving God, a loving God, a long-suffering God.

These things are all characteristics of God. We must remember, however, that God's characteristics never make Him God, but because He is God, His characteristics will never change. God is who He is all the time. He doesn't change, and therefore He must judge according to His perfect standard. Since God judges according to this standard, we are condemned to eternal judgment before a perfect God. When we stand in judgment before Him, we are absolutely helpless to defend ourselves from His righteous wrath. The price must be paid!

The passage from John's first epistle comes into play at this point. Because God so loves His creation, because God is long-suffering and forgiving, He allowed someone else to endure His wrath on our behalf. Scripture says Jesus "is the propitiation for our sins." *Propitiate* means to appease or to atone.

Considering that God's standard is perfection and that all have sinned, missing the mark, someone had to live perfectly to satisfy the divine standard. Scripture says that somebody was Jesus. Not only did He live perfectly, but He died perfectly. Many of us may believe that God let us escape punishment and get away with sin. In fact, Jesus took the punishment for our sins. God's righteous and justified wrath was poured out on Jesus while He hung on the cross. As one scholar said,, "Propitiation stresses that the holiness of God was fully satisfied, His wrath appeased, and His righteous demands were met through the atoning death of Christ." So, Christian, your propitiation was fulfilled in the death of your Savior. Rejoice in the fact that when you couldn't, He could.

Pray and thank God for the death of His Son, Jesus. Thank Him that He loved you enough to allow Jesus to take your place.

NOTES

Day Five: Mercies of God

"Therefore, brothers, by the mercies of God, I urge you to present your bodies as a living sacrifice, holy and pleasing to God; this is your spiritual worship" (Rom. 12:1 Holman CSB).

Every one of us can be thankful for God's mercy. His mercy allows us to accept His divine grace. Mercy means God won't give us what we deserve. Have you ever told a lie? Certainly you have. According to Revelation 21:8, all liars go to hell. That's what you deserve. But God had mercy on us. That doesn't mean that God will allow everyone to go to heaven. Because of His holiness, He couldn't possibly do that.. However, His mercy gives us the opportunity to accept Jesus as our Savior.

This verse is written to those who have accepted God's gift of grace by faith. The apostle Paul beckons these Christians to offer their bodies as living sacrifices. He urges them to do so. It's a strong appeal to live their lives separate from the world order and in obedience to Christ and His commands. However, before he tells them to do that, he asks them to view their lives through God's mercy.

I can remember watching a 3-D movie when I was a child. When I put on those glasses, things looked different. The big screen seemed to jump out at me. Looking through those glasses made me respond to the movie in a new way. Paul is asking us to put on the 3-D glasses of God's mercy, then live our lives according to the mercy we've been given.

Can you remember doing something bad when you were a small child? You knew you deserved a whipping, but your parents displayed mercy, warning you and giving you a second chance. Didn't that act of mercy alter the way you viewed your parents for the rest of the day? You gladly obeyed their every command. Paul is simply reminding Christians to see how merciful God has been to us, with the hopeful expectation that we will react to that mercy and joyfully offer our bodies as living sacrifices.

Can you think of how God has had mercy on you? God's mercy ushered in salvation for you. How else has His mercy affected your life? Can you look at your life and say, "I'll offer my body as a living sacrifice, because God was so merciful to me"? Pray and thank God for His mercy and grace in your life. Ask Him to help you see His mercy so that you will remain faithful to Him.

NOTES

Day Six: Jars of clay

"Now we have this treasure in clay jars, so that this extraordinary power may be from God and not from us" (2 Cor. 4:7 Holman CSB).

Some people seem to have vitally important jobs. Think about the president of the United States. How important is his job? He must consider himself very fortunate to hold such a position. However, the Christian has the most important position of any person on earth. That's because we have a message with the power to change more than the world. It changes eternity! This message is a priceless treasure to the lost soul.

Paul declares in this passage that we are like jars of clay containing treasure. In Bible days, people would often store their valuables in clay pots. Paul uses this imagery to illustrate the relationship between Christians and the gospel. Paul said in Romans 1:16 that the gospel has power unto salvation. The treasure that we carry is the death, burial, and resurrection of the Lord Jesus Christ.

I'm amazed that Christ would trust me with this message.

After all, I'm just a clay pot. To understand the significance of clay pots, we must understand their qualities. They were ordinary earthen vessels and could have been worn and cracked. The jar wasn't anything special, just a carrier of something special. Without the treasure, it was just another clay pot.

What is Paul trying to say here? Simply this: God has saved us by His precious Son, Jesus Christ. He desires for all men to be saved. He doesn't require that you be a magnificent person to be saved. In other words, He wants to use ordinary people to carry His message to the world. God does this so that He might get the glory. This plan is all about lifting up the Father in heaven. Ordinary people take a powerful, godly message and spread it to the world. God does extraordinary work through the message, and people glorify Him because of it.

Our lives should never point people to us. They should always point to God. How precious it is to know that God trusts me with a message that changes eternity. May He get all the praise for it! Let us remember that we are just clay pots carrying God's special message.

Pray and thank God for trusting you with the gospel of Christ. Ask Him to help you point people to Him and not to yourself.

Notes

Day Seven: Treasures in heaven

"Do not lay up for yourselves treasures on earth, where moth and rust destroy and where thieves break in and steal, but lay up for yourselves treasure in heaven, where neither moth nor rust destroys and where thieves do not break in and steal. For where your treasure is, there you heart will be also" (Matt. 6:19–21).

On walls, in closets, and in cabinets at my house are various treasures. I have the Bible my grandfather received in war. I also have his pocketknife. I have the autographs of a few famous football players and baseballs from professional players. I have a baseball card worth five hundred dollars.

Other things that I have bought are treasures to me. A treasure is something of great value. It doesn't have to be expensive to be a treasure. The uniqueness makes it a treasure. Treasure doesn't have to be material. It can be a memory or a special place that you adore. What happens if a thief steals your treasure? You may never recover material treasure. And what if you suffer amnesia and can't remember treasures of the heart? They are gone.

There is one treasure, however, that can never be stolen or taken away. It's the treasure of the gospel of Jesus Christ living inside of us. This treasure should be valued more than anything that we could ever buy or remember. This treasure is so valuable because it's the only thing that can save man from his sin debt. The things of this world will pass away, but the gospel will remain for eternity.

Thank God every day for the treasure that He's given you, one that thieves can't have, rust can't overtake, and moths can't destroy. There's no treasure like the treasure given by Christ Jesus. Pray and thank God for this beautiful treasure. Ask Him to help you value it more than anything you could ever receive.

NOTES

Day Eight: Having a bad day

When you are having a bad day, what do you do to overcome it? Scripture teaches us that Peter had a bad day. On the day of the Lord's arrest, Peter denied Jesus three times. After the third denial, Peter wept because he knew in his heart that he had let the Lord down. Don't you feel that way when you have a bad day? Maybe you got angry with a coworker or yelled at your children. The moments following those occasions are tough to deal with. Somehow we've let our circumstances influence us to behave inappropriately.

So how do we recover? Peter later shows us what we need to do to reconcile with God and have a great day. The story is found in chapter 21 of John's gospel. Jesus had been raised from the grave, and the disciples had returned to their everyday activities. They were fishing. Peter was well aware that the last time he saw Jesus alive he denied Him. As the disciples fished, Jesus walked on the seashore. Jesus told them to cast their net on the other side of the boat and they would catch some fish. He had done this before. They obeyed and caught plenty.

At this point, they recognized the risen Lord. Peter jumped from the boat and sped toward Jesus. The Bible says the disciples had caught so many fish that it took seven men to drag the net to shore. But after Jesus told them to bring the fish to Him, Peter dragged the net by himself. He seemed to be doing everything possible to show his Father that he loved Him. Peter wanted to make up for the bad day he'd had by trying to please his Father.

There's our answer to a bad day. Do whatever it takes to please the Father. Our Father wouldn't want us to be angry with others or scream at our children or do anything else that hurts people. When we hurt others, we hurt Him. So go to those whom you have hurt, apologize, and thank God that He loves you and them. Surely this will help turn your day from sour to superb. It takes a great deal of courage to admit you are wrong, but Peter was willing to do whatever it took. And we should be, too. Pray and ask God to help you remember this truth when you're having a bad day.

NOTES

Day Nine: God's grace

"For by grace you have been saved through faith, and this is not from yourselves; it is God's gift" (Eph. 2:8 Holman CSB).

Here's a great question. What is it about your life that would make God love you? Is it your beauty, your money, or your popularity? Maybe He loves you because you do many things of which He approves. In fact, God's love depends on none of those things. Though you may be doing things that Christ finds commendable, that's not why He loves you. He loves you because He can't help but love you. The Bible says God is love. He loves you simply because it's His character to love you, and love doesn't know how to do anything but love. Even on the worst day of your life, God still loves you.

It's this kind of love that allows God to extend His saving grace to unworthy people like you and me. God's grace is rooted in His unending love. It's not that God has to love us; it's simply that He wants to love us. A great definition for *grace* is God's want-to, not His have-to. The Bible says that we are saved because of this grace and love. God reminds us in this verse that it's not about us. If it were about us, God's grace would be useless because we could earn salvation by works. Simply put, God is saying, "You can't be good enough to be saved, but that's okay because I love you enough to save you even when you don't deserve it."

In this verse, we find the highway leading to salvation. It's found in the word *faith*. In whom must you have faith? It must be in Jesus Christ. Though God loves everyone, people must put their faith in Jesus Christ to be saved from their sins. "For by grace you have been saved through faith, and this is not from yourselves; it is God's gift."

Wow! What a gift! What amazing love, what amazing grace that Christ would love a wretch like me. I once was lost, but now I'm found, was blind but now I see. God, I thank you for your amazing love and amazing grace.

NOTES

Day Ten: God's hand upon us

"The gracious hand of his God was on him, because Ezra had determined in his heart to study the law of the Lord, obey it, and teach its statutes and ordinances in Israel" (Ezra 7:9–10 Holman CSB).

All who belong to Christ desire to have God's blessings follow them. Everyone wants to be able to say at the end of the day, God has been with me! This passage says that God's hand was upon Ezra's life. To have the hand of God upon you simply means that His guidance is with you. Scripture mentions seven times that the hand of the Lord was on Ezra. To say the least, Ezra was guided by God in leading the Israelites.

God's guiding hand will lead us in the right direction no matter what the situation. We must remember that God created our lives for His glory, so why not let Him guide us? But how do we get God to place His hand upon us? God had a plan and purpose for His people, and Ezra was going to lead the Israelites back to that plan and purpose. It was Ezra's job to make sure he was leading them in the right direction. The Bible says Ezra made up his mind to follow three principles. First, he devoted himself to studying God's Word. Second, he devoted himself to obeying God's Word. Third, he devoted his heart to teaching others all he had learned from God's Word. The Bible says that because he did this, God's hand was upon him.

It's critical that we see the driving factor in having God's hand upon us. Gaining this grace begins with the Word of God, our source of guidance and strength. When we devote our hearts to studying it, obeying it, and teaching it, God will graciously guide us into His truth and into His plan. Make up your mind today that you will spend more time being devoted to God's Word so you can be guided by His gracious hand.

NOTES

Printed in the United States
By Bookmasters